EXPLORE MICHIGAN
TRAVERSE CITY

George Cantor has been a journalist in the Detroit area for more than 40 years. He worked for the *Detroit Free Press* and the *Detroit News* as a baseball writer, travel writer, reporter and columnist.

His proudest achievements were covering the 1968 Detroit Tigers in their championship season, raising two beautiful daughters and seeing columns he had written years ago still hanging on refrigerator doors around the state.

He also has written 15 books on sports, travel and history.

George and his wife Sherry are residents of West Bloomfield, along with their irascible west highland terrier, Charlie.

EXPLORE MICHIGAN

TRAVERSE CITY

An Insider's Guide to Michigan

George Cantor

The University of Michigan Press
Ann Arbor
&
Petoskey Publishing Company
Traverse City

Published in the United States of America by
The University of Michigan Press
Manufactured in the United States of America
Printed on acid-free paper

2008   2007   2006   2005   4   3   2   1

ISBN 0-472-03091-4

Library of Congress Cataloging-in-publication Data on File

Cover photograph provided by
Marge Beaver, Photography Plus,
www.photography-plus.com

Inside photography courtesy of
John Russell,
www.tcphoto.com

CONTENTS

Explore Michigan: An Insider's Guide to Michigan is not meant to be a complete listing of every restaurant or every shop; it is truly meant to be an "insider's" guide. It recommends the places that the locals, and in the case of the tourist areas, long-time summer residents, know about, frequent and recommend to their family and friends.

For example, in Traverse City, the parking meters have a button that you can hit for thirty free minutes. In Leelanau County, the National Park Service conducts winter snowshoe tours of the park. In Detroit, there are cozy restaurants that out-of-towners rarely find. And if you want a more affordable, and quiet weekend at the Grand Hotel on Mackinac Island, it is now open in early spring.

Author George Cantor has been writing travel books for over twenty years. A life-long Michigander, he has traveled and explored Michigan with the gusto it takes to make these books special. Though they are guidebooks, they make for a good read before, during and after you plan to visit. George also wanted to make sure that he really had the local flare for each book in this series, so he agreed to have locals review each book and give their comments to him.

The result is *Explore Michigan: An Insider's Guide to Michigan*, where the aerial photographs on the covers by exceptionally talented Marge Beaver invite you in. Once you start reading, you are on your way to invaluable information that puts you on the inside of what our great state has to offer.

--the publishers

TRAVERSE CITY

The Top Ten Don't Miss List

1. Drive or bike to the top of Old Mission Peninsula.
2. Attend a concert at Interlochen.
3. Explore the classic Victorian homes along historic Sixth Street.
4. Stroll and shop downtown's Front Street.
5. Stop for a super thick milk shake at Don's Drive-in.
6. Walk through the zoo and marina at Clinch Park.
7. Visit one of the Old Mission wineries.
8. Stop at a farm market for some of the finest fruit in the Midwest.
9. Wade in the water at one of the beaches on the bay.
10. Take a cross-country ski trip through Pere Marquette State Forest.

THE TURF

A view from the Park Place Hotel

It may be the most dramatic location of any city in Michigan.

Tucked in between two ranges of hills, at the base of a sparkling bay, resort hotels lined up along its beaches. Traverse City lives up to its reputation as the Great Lakes Riviera.

But it is more than just a pretty face.

While it may sound improbable to use the words "city" and "northern Michigan" in the same sentence, Traverse City is a fully realized urban entity.

Its downtown is among the most diverse in the state. Its range of entertainment options is surprisingly wide. It has become a home for affluent retirees as well as young people who don't want to sacrifice quality of life for sophisticated amenities.

It has a new airport that is world class, opening in 2004 to rave reviews.

The city proper remains rather small, with under 18,000 residents. But the growth in surrounding Grand Traverse County has made it the most populous in the north.

The best entrance is coming in from the north, along

U.S. 31 or Michigan 22. The roads sweep in along either arm of Grand Traverse Bay, with the long slender finger of Old Mission Peninsula beckoning across the water. Especially in the early evening, when the lights start to flicker on in the beachfront resorts and the waterfront homes on the Peninsula, it is a magical sight.

The name of the bay and the county betrays the area's origins. Grand Traverse was named the "long crossing" by French explorers and trappers in the late 17th Century. It was the shortcut from the Leelanau Peninsula to the mainland across the mouth of the bay.

The first American settler arrived in 1839, when Rev. Peter Dougherty made the crossing to set up a Presbyterian mission on the peninsula which divides the great bay in two. The entire peninsula became named for his mission church.

The minister is also credited with being the first to see the potential of the bay area for growing fruit. The local cherry industry, which now supplies nearly 75 percent of the tart varieties grown in the United States, had its genesis in an orchard he planted near his mission in 1852.

But by treaty with the Odawa, his parishioners could not own land on the Old Mission Peninsula. So later that same year he decided to return to the Leelanau, and the great cherry boom had to wait another few decades.

It was lumber that made the first fortunes. Horace Boardman came to the future Traverse City seven years after Dougherty, and by 1847 he had built the first sawmill along the river that now bears his name.

Two Chicago investors, Perry Hannah and Albert Lay, arrived in 1851 and began laying out the city as a base for their expanded lumbering operations. Over the next 35 years, they would process 400 million board feet. A hint of the riches built on those pine boards can be seen in the massive Victorian homes that rose along Sixth Street between 1890 and 1900.

The partnership of Hannah and Lay was the greatest economic force in the area, also running a steamship service to Chicago and Traverse City's biggest store.

By the 1890s, though, the lumber industry was in unmistakable decline. Other northern lumbering towns never recovered from that downturn. But Traverse City found an alternative. The sandy soil and sheltering hills that had made Rev. Dougherty's
orchard successful were still there.

In 1893, near the site of the original planting, the area's first commercial cherry enterprise, Ridgewood Farm, went into operation. Within ten years, cherry production had outstripped all other crops in the area and a new boom had begun. By 1924 Traverse City was saluting its big crop with the Blessing of the Blossoms. This has since grown into the National Cherry Festival, one of the great summertime attractions in the Great Lakes area.

A few visionaries wondered if you could grow world-class cherries here, why not grapes? In the 1980s, they opened the first wineries on the Old Mission Peninsula, and that has become a second important source of agricultural income.

The explosive growth of Traverse City has wiped out some of the older orchards. But all you have to do is drive a little bit farther out on the Peninsula and you will soon be surrounded by the rolling farmland and blooming acres that are Grand Traverse's special grace.

Inside one of the barns on the grounds of the Commons

THE TOWNS

Winter in downtown Traverse City is beautiful

Traverse City. The city grew up along the mouth of a lumbering stream, the Boardman River, where it entered Grand Traverse Bay. The river still runs downtown, although in places it's tucked away like an eccentric relative, separating parking lots from the main shopping district along Front Street.

The river also is the dividing line between downtown and Old Town, a neighborhood of magnificent lumber-era homes and a few rakish saloons along Union Street.

Beaches and marinas are just a few steps from the heart of the business district, which gives Traverse City the sense of a place that is always half ready to go on vacation. A string of inland lakes a short drive south of the city adds to the resort-like feeling.

Interlochen. There is nothing like it in America, a summer camp for the fine arts that has shaped this country's musical heritage for the last 70 years. Ten percent of the seats in the country's symphony orchestras are occupied by its alumni. Originally intended as a place for talented high school musicians, it has expanded to embrace dance, theater and visual arts and an academy that is a year-round boarding school.

Situated, as the name promises, on a neck of land between two lakes southwest of Traverse City, Interlochen welcomes visitors to tour its grounds, attend its concerts and sit in on its rehearsals. It's an experience that shouldn't be missed.

Old Mission. This is the site of Rev. Peter Dougherty's mission, the first permanent European settlement in the area. It is in the tranquil northeastern corner of the Old Mission Peninsula, with a reconstructed version of the log mission, an old general store, quiet beaches and a good deal of serenity.

Acme. If Old Mission is the old face of the Grand Traverse area, Acme is the new. Once a quiet crossroads on the east bay, it was transformed into a bustling suburban strip by the opening of the Grand Traverse Resort and its splendid golf courses in the early 1980s. The Turtle Creek Casino is four miles east on M-72.

LOCAL COLOR

Cherries

You cannot help but notice that they grow an awful lot of cherries around here. You'll find the name on the airport, a mall, downtown businesses, the annual local festival. You'll see the fruit for sale at numerous roadside stands, on the menu in various forms at local restaurants, in everything from pies to hamburgers. If the old song is true and life really is just a bowl of cherries, then Traverse City is the table it sits upon.

It is the tart cherry that rules. In other parts of the world, it goes by the name of sour cherry. But the Grand

Cherries are a Traverse City staple

Traverse growers decided long ago that 'sour' had too many negative connotations. So they prefer 'tart'. Whatever you call them, the Grand Traverse area grows more than 70% of this variety in America, primarily the Montmorency. About two-thirds of that crop is frozen for use in pie filling and preserves.

This red fruit has been around for a very long time. There is evidence of sweet cherry cultivation in parts of the Middle East going back 3,000 years. It probably originated in the mountainous plateaus of Turkey and Iran, and still is an agricultural staple in those countries.

The tart variety is a bit more recent in origin. Botanists believe it came into Eastern Europe somewhere around 300 B.C., when sweet cherries and a shrub called ground cherry intermingled. The ancient Greeks knew of it and made it part of their diet, and it was also a preferred food of the Roman legions.

Cherry blossoms

Cherries have been made into tea, liqueurs, soup, and wine. British poet A.E. Housman called it, "the loveliest of trees." You also hear it in the words of old folk songs; "I gave my love a cherry that had no stone," and, "Can she bake a cherry pie, Darlin' Billy?"

The fruit spread westward very slowly, not arriving in England until the Norman Invasion of 1066. British colonists then completed the global circuit by planting trees in New England and around the Great Lakes. It was only the tart variety, however, that was hearty enough to survive the harsh North American winters.

The chokecherry is indigenous to this area, though. Even before the first cherry tree was planted in Michigan, the Ojibwa were using this shrub to relieve throat irritations that accompanied coughs. It later became a principal ingredient in the manufacture of cough drops and may also be effective in treating kidney disorders.

And, of course, it was a cherry tree that young George Washington chopped down in the tale concocted by a later biographer to show the future President's propensity for always telling the truth. The cherry has proven more enduring than that political attribute.

Perry Hannah

Few people have left as deep an imprint on their community as this pioneering businessman did on Traverse City.

When he arrived by schooner from Chicago in 1851, the place consisted of a sawmill on the Boardman River. At his death, 53 years later, he was revered as the father of a city.

Hannah was the quintessential timber baron. The wealth of white pine in the hills and forests of the area and the easy water transportation to get them to market put dollar signs in his eyes when he arrived. But he also saw more. The natural beauty of Grand Traverse Bay charmed him and unlike many of his colleagues he wanted to build something lasting on that.

In a passage of his memoirs, written late in life, he recalled his first glimpse of the future city's site. He rounded the tip of Old Mission Peninsula just as the sun was setting and saw a group of Indian hunters on the shore watching his ship. He wrote, "A more beautiful picture I never

The original Perry Hannah house today is a funeral home

saw in my life."

Hannah had come to buy the sawmill and adjacent 200 acres of land, the foundation of his fortune and that of his principal partner, Albert Lay. Traverse City rose on that acreage and when it was incorporated in 1881 Hannah was the first village president.

At the northwest corner of the main downtown intersection, which is now Front and Union, Hannah and Lay opened the town's first bank. Their general store, the largest commercial emporium in the north, rose on the northeast corner. They bought and enlarged the first hotel, the core of today's luxurious Park Place.

Hannah helped build the city's opera house, which was recently restored. Through his considerable political influence, the State was persuaded to locate the Northern Michigan Asylum here in 1885, and it became one of the city's leading employers.

All of these places still stand, although some have been adapted to other uses. Hannah's own home, a 34-room civic landmark on Sixth Street, completed in 1893, is now a funeral home and gives tours by appointment.

Dr. James Decker Munson

He was 37 years old when he was named medical superintendent of the new Northern Michigan Asylum in 1885. He found the site to be a morass of tree stumps and barren ground. That suited Munson just fine. He had some strong ideas about effective treatment of the mentally ill, and the condition of the land would enable him to shape it according to his theories. He was something of a prodigy, making a reputation as one of the finest neurologists in Detroit just a few years after graduation from the University of Michigan School of Medicine.

Building 50 - an architectural masterpiece

Munson deplored the harsh, prison-like surroundings to which most mental hospitals relegated their patients. He believed that a beautiful setting would enhance medical treatment and he began turning these grounds into a garden.

He collected seeds for flowers, trees and shrubs while on his travels and oversaw their planting here. The asylum structures, especially the ornate Victorian-Italianate "Building 50," were also designed with aesthetic qualities in mind. The entire complex was closed in 1989 and is now being developed as a mixed-use village within a city, Grand Traverse Commons. Building 50 is to be its centerpiece.

Munson also established the city's first general hospital in 1915, and it is still in operation as the Munson Medical Center. The portion of U.S. 31 that sweeps along the base of the bay's eastern arm, past the largest concentration of resort hotels, is named Munson Avenue in his honor.

Dr. Joseph Maddy and Interlochen

"The Music Man" was the story of a smooth-talking con man and his efforts to dupe an Iowa town by selling band instruments its children couldn't play. But the real Music Man was named Joseph E. Maddy, and his work with young artists changed the course of American musical history.

Interlochen was Maddy's vision, "A dream city of youth…where beauty reigns and where talented young people gather for inspiration."

The Kansas-born Maddy was trained in the violin and played briefly with the Minneapolis Symphony. His real vocation however was teaching music. He built a reputation for excellence in the public schools of Rochester, N.Y., and in 1926 organized a National High School Orchestra. Its success led to the founding of Interlochen two years later.

At first it was intended as a summer camp for members of that orchestra. But over the years it has expanded to fulfill Maddy's description of a dream city, with a summer population of more than 3,000 young artists. They come from every state and 40 foreign countries to learn, create and be inspired.

Contemporary pop artists such as Jewel, Norah Jones and Josh Groban are alumni. So are newsman Mike Wallace, opera star Jessye Norman, conductor Lorin Maazel, cartoonist Cathy Guisewite, composer Peter Yarrow, and thousands of professional musicians and educators around the world.

WHERE TO STAY

The Grand Traverse Resort

Top of the Line

Grand Traverse Resort. U.S. 31 north of M-72, Acme. (800) 748-0303.

At its opening in 1980, the Grand Traverse was regarded as pretty risky business. There was no previous evidence that this area could support a full-scale luxury resort built around golf. Even the idea of bringing in Jack Nicklaus to design its signature course, the Bear, was a gamble.

The original developer, Bloomfield Hills attorney Paul Nine, told the story of walking the property with Nicklaus and coming to the top of a rise with a fine view over the bay. "What a great hole this will make," said Nine. "No, this is too beautiful to be part of a golf course," Nicklaus responded. "You've got to put condos here."

He was right, of course, and after a few financial mishaps Grand Traverse got it right, too. It is the most complete four-season resort in northern Michigan, with an indoor recreation complex and spa matching the quality of its golf, which now includes three courses.

Its seventeen story hotel tower is the tallest building in

the area. There are 460 standard hotel rooms and another 198 condo units and suites.

The resort is now owned by the Grand Traverse Band of Ottawa and Chippewa and has free shuttle service to the nearby Turtle Creek Casino, which the tribes also operate.

Park Place Hotel. 300 East State Street, Traverse City. (800) 748-0133.

This inn goes right back to the roots of Traverse City. The original opened in 1873, as the Campbell House, before the town was even incorporated. Five years later, it was sold to the city's leading businessmen, the Hannah-Lay partnership.

The inside of the Park Place

They upgraded the property to make it a community showcase and renamed it for the park on which it was then situated. The hotel has undergone renovation several times since then. The most significant was in 1930 when its ten story tower was completed, and that is still the core of the present-day hotel.

There are 137 rooms, plus three balcony suites on the second and top ninth floor with views over the bay. The Beacon Lounge occupies the top floor with a spectacular view out over the bay. Although it is located in the middle of downtown, the Park Place has package deal arrangements with several area golf courses and wineries and is only steps from the beach.

Especially for Kids

Great Wolf Lodge. U.S. 31 South, Traverse City. (866) GR8-WOLF.
An indoor waterpark built within an all-suite hotel, this is an interesting choice for family groups, especially in the colder months. Passes to the four-story high park are free to guests, and include access to eight giant water slides and

The popular Great Wolf Lodge

five pools. There is also a game arcade and a spa for water-logged adults.

The Great Wolf Lodge opened in 2003 and is among the first in the country to be started up by this national resort company. Rates for suites start at $259.

Sleeping with History

Country Hermitage. 7710 U.S. 31 North, Acme. (231) 938-5930. Built as a farmhouse in 1883, this Bed and Breakfast remains at the center of a working 400-acre cherry farm. The hilltop location opens out on bay views from all six rooms, and in May, when the surrounding orchards are in bloom, it is surrounded by a pink sea.

Nels and Michelle Veliquette opened the inn after extensive restoration work in 1999. Their favorite room is the Pulcipher, named after the family who built the house. All rooms have private bath and central air, and rates run from $110 to $198 a night.

Neahtawanta Inn. Old Mission Peninsula, left from Peninsula Drive on Neahtawanta Road. (800) 220-1415.

The inn was built as a summer home in 1885 and became a hotel 21 years later. After some vicissitudes in the 1970s, it was purchased by Sally Van Vleck and Bob Russell, a couple who operate the five-room B&B on a basis of environmental respect and peace activism.

It emphasizes the natural beauty of its surroundings and the opportunity for contemplation, including a yoga studio. Try Room 4, which has a full view of lovely Bowers Harbor and a private bathroom. (Two of the rooms share that facility.) Rates range from $100 for a double room to $175 for a suite.

Yorkburg Manor. 5721 N. Broomhead Road, south from M-72, Williamsburg. (877) 310-9675.

This old farmhouse is truly a survivor. Boarded up and slated for demolition in the 1990s to make way for a big box commercial development, it was rescued by John and Judy York. They moved it 5 miles to a serene location at the edge of Pere Marquette State Forest.

Built in 1896 on a dairy farm, the manor is a good location for those who are seeking a retreat close to hiking, cross-country ski trails and the Sand Lake Quiet Area of the state forest. There are four rooms, and the two that share a bath can be combined as a suite. The Roger/Dennis Room features its own fireplace, too. Rates start at $110 and go to $135 a night.

Sleeping with Wine

Chateau Chantal. Old Mission Peninsula, off M-37,

north of Mapleton. (800) 969-4009

The owners of this winery like to point out that it is located on the same line of latitude as the famed Bordeaux region of France. Chateau Chantal is somewhat younger, however, beginning operations in 1983.

Because of its location on a ridge, the chateau opens out on views across the vineyards to both arms of Grand Traverse Bay. The inn offers eleven rooms; two standard bedrooms, eight suites and a two-bedroom executive apartment.

Weekend rates during the high season, May through October, range from $145 for a standard room to $185 for a suite with a two-night minimum. Midweek rates are lower.

Grey Hare Inn. Old Mission Peninsula, right from M-37 on Carroll Road, near Peninsula Cellars. (800) 873-0652.

Situated in a rustic farmhouse in the midst of a working vineyard, the inn comes as close to the country French experience as this side of the Atlantic allows. There is a tasting room right down the lane as well as walking trails through seventeen acres of vineyards and woods.

There are three inn rooms, all of them furnished in the manner of a Burgundy farmhouse. Try the Grange de Bois with its grape trellis bed, French doors and private fireplace. Two-night minimums apply for weekends between July and October.

Other Choices

The waterfront resorts line up side by side along U.S. 31 as it runs along the base of Grand Traverse Bay. All of them feature sand beaches (although unusually low water levels in recent years have required extensive grooming) and indoor pools.

The most impressive cluster is on the bay's eastern arm. The Cherry Tree Inn on the Beach, Grand Beach and Sugar Beach offer good value at around $150 a night. They are all especially kid-friendly, too.

Camping

Traverse City State Park truly is a park within the city. In reality, the city grew out to surround the park, which was formed in 1920 on 15 acres of played out timber land. Further acquisitions tripled the original size by 1939.

The 342-site campground on U.S. 31 runs year-round. There is access to a Grand Traverse Bay beach on the far side of the highway. The park also connects to the TART biking and hiking trail, which runs across the city. Modern bath facilities operate from April to December. This is a very popular facility and advance reservations are necessary. Call (231) 922-5270.

There was a state park at **Interlochen** even before there was a music camp. It is the oldest such facility in Michigan's Lower Peninsula, established in 1917, and was intended to preserve a stand of virgin white pine. Eleven years later, the National Music Camp went into business right next door, making this 187-acre facility a paradise for those who love the outdoors and great music.

Interlochen has 490 campsites. The Duck Lake campground is the most modern with 428 sites, and there are 62 rustic accommodations at Green Lake. There is also a short nature trail, exhibits on logging, a beach, store and excel

lent cross-country skiing. The park is located on M-137 adjacent to the main entrance to the Music Camp. Again, advance reservations are imperative. Call (231) 276-9511.

Five primitive campgrounds are scattered around the **Pere Marquette State Forest** in Grand Traverse County. Two of them are on the Boardman River, southeast of Traverse City. The Boardman is a good trout stream and both of these campgrounds have boat ramps.

Scheck's Place, with thirty campsites, links up with the state forest's Muncie Lakes riding and hiking trail. **Forks** has only eight campsites in an even more secluded stretch of the river. Both are reached by driving south from Traverse City on Garfield Road, then left on Brown Bridge Road.

Spring Lake, in the southeastern corner of the county, has thirty-two sites on the lake of the same name. It is just off U.S. 131, south of the town of Fife Lake.

In the Interlochen area is the **Lake Dubonnet Campground,** with fifty sites on the water and links to the Lost Lake Nature Pathway. From Interlochen, take M-137 north, left on U.S. 31, then right on Lake Dubonnet Road.

A favorite of local campers is **Arbutus #4,** on a beautiful inland lake with an outstanding swimming beach. There are twenty-three sites here. Take Garfield Road south from the city, then left on Potter Road to the campground.

As with all state forest campgrounds, no reservations are accepted.

Timber Ridge Campground and Nordic Center is a good choice for RV'ers. It has 230 sites, an outdoor swimming pool and a location convenient to both the city and cross country skiing areas. Follow Three Mile Road south from the city, then left, to 4050 Hammond Road. (231) 947-2770.

Closer to the Interlochen area is **Holiday Park,** another option for the RV crowd. It is located on the shores of Silver Lake, just off U.S. 31, about midway between Traverse City and the Music Camp. Open April through November. (231) 943-4410.

EATING OUT

Orchards and vineyards surround the city and its restaurants reflect the quality of local produce. Fruits and vegetables are right off the farm with a degree of freshness that is increasingly hard to find in a freeze-wrapped world. The waters of Grand Traverse Bay and the neighboring inland lakes and streams are renowned for their whitefish, trout and walleye.

Eight Evenings Out

Bowers Harbor Inn. 13512 Peninsula Drive, Old Mission Peninsula. (231) 223-4222. This reliable standby is famous for its whitefish-in-a-bag dinners, although its menu ranges much further afield than that. The place was built in the 1880s by the Stickneys, a wealthy Chicago family.

Two popular restaurants on Old Mission

According to legend, the wife of the builder still hangs around to spook guests by popping up in mirrors. The restaurant also bottles wine from its own vineyards.

This is a delightfully, softly sophisticated, old fashioned sort of Up North place and it shouldn't be missed.

The Boathouse. 14039 Peninsula Drive, Old Mission Peninsula. (231) 223-4030. On a marina just up the road from Bowers Harbor, it has the added advantage of sitting right on the West Arm of the bay with views of the harbor and Power Island. The food matches the setting, too, with outstanding fish and duck dishes. There is also a big fireplace for the days when the wind comes whipping off the water.

The restaurant is open for lunch and is a good choice during day trips to the historic sights and wineries on the Peninsula.

A popular Traverse City restaurant

Mode's Bum Steer. 125 E. State Street, downtown.
(231) 947-9832. The locals know value and so they stand
in line on weekends, even when the weather turns nippy, to
dig into the black angus steaks that are Mode's specialty. The
restaurant has been in operation since 1974, but the building
is much older than that. It observed its centennial in 2004
(first opening as Hoolihan's Bar) and passed through a variety of incarnations, including a burger joint and a Prohibition
era coffee shop, before taking its present form.

The room is tiny, the tables are a bit tightly packed but
this is a good square meal with a warm ambience.

310. 310 S. Cass Street. (231) 932-1310. Sitting right
across the Boardman River from downtown, this is an
imaginative operation in a new office-residential development. A wide assortment of appetizers, individual pizzas
and sushi make up the core of the menu, or you can also
order a full-course dinner.

The bar is active and stays open late for Traverse's
bright young things. In warm weather there is outdoor dining above the river.

Amical. 229 E. Front Street, downtown.
(231) 941-8888. A classic bistro in the heart of the shopping

area, Amical is a little slice of Gallic heaven. Great quiche and extraordinary desserts. Views of the river from its rear windows and outdoor seating (complete with overhead heaters for chilly evenings) to take in the traffic on Front in front.

During the off-season, its chefs work up monthly regional menus from different areas of France.

Hanna's. 118 Cass St., Traverse City. 231 946-8207.
The former owners of Hattie's in Sutton's Bay opened this new entry in northern fine dining late in 2004. They look on it as a fresh start in a new place, but the emphasis remains on seafood and a wide assortment of good but moderately priced wines. In the heart of downtown.

Windows. 7677 West Bay Shore Drive (M-22) (231) 941-0100. Technically, we're over the line and into Leelanau County here. But the restaurants along the west bayshore are so much a part of Traverse City that it would be indefensible to omit them.

Besides, many residents will tell you that Windows is the top dining experience in the area. Or, at least, the most romantic. Smashing view, candlelight, Cajun-style cuisine, and most extensive wine list. Probably the priciest choice, too, but the quality matches the tariff.

Old Mission Tavern. 17015 M-37, Old Mission Peninsula. (231) 223-7280. Art on the walls, sculptures in the gardens and prime rib in the kitchen. How can you beat it? Under the ownership of sculptor Verna Bartnick, this is as much an art gallery as a restaurant, but the quality of the food is not slighted.

Trattoria Stella ("star"). Cottage View Drive, (11th St.), which is Building 50 in Grand Traverse Commons. (231) 929-8989. Bldg 50. Owner Paul Danielson had experience in a number of Detroit restaurants, and his wife Amanda was director of training for Elias Brothers Corporation, so one would expect excellent service. Their chef came from the Townsend Hotel in Birmingham. Everything is made from scratch, and seafood is flown in five days a week. The menu changes twice daily. Opened in the summer of 2004, this is a hot spot for locals.

An Insider's Tip

The Great Lakes Culinary Institute is one of the Midwest's finest, located on the Great Lakes campus of Northwestern Michigan College (just east of downtown, off Front Street near the Holiday Inn). Its 90-seat training restaurant serves lunch and dinner during the school year. The prices are a major bargain and the view over the bay is spectacular. Reservations are a must. (231) 995-3120

Informal Places

Omelette Shoppe. Two downtown locations, at 124 Cass (231-946-0912) and 1209 E. Front. (231-946-0590). A breakfast tradition in this city. As the name implies, eggs are the big attraction here, although the bake shop serves up a stellar array of pastries. The Cass Street location is surrounded by city and county offices and you may well be sitting across the booth from someone you read about in that morning's *Record-Eagle*.

Don's Drive-in. 2030 U.S. 31 North, East Bayfront. (231) 938-1860. Put your glad rags on and join me, hon, where the 50s never left. The burgers, the shakes you eat with a spoon, the old time rock n'roll on the jukebox. One of Traverse City's traditional spots and a place for the truly hungry.

Mabel's. 472 Munson, East Bayfront. (231) 947-0252. Another breakfast hot spot in the middle of the hotel district. A great family choice for reasons of both menu and price, although on summer weekends there will be a wait.

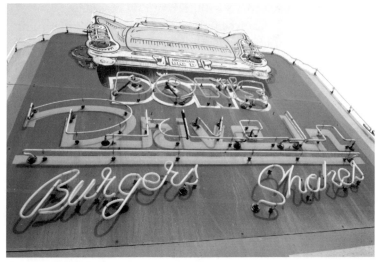

A step back in time

Hofbrau. M-137, just north of Interlochen. (231) 276-6979.
Road-house style food at the most convenient restaurant to
the Interlochen concert venues. It's in an old general store,
with an extensive menu. The ribs and frog legs go down best.

Giovanni's. 9205 US 31, Grawn. (231) 276-6244.
Another wonderful restaurant near Interlochen. As the
name implies, it is Italian and has a great low key atmosphere, good food and good prices.

Apache Trout Grill. 13671 South West Bay Shore Drive
(M-22). (231) 947-7079. A casual alternative to Windows
along the scenic west bayfront, this is a very popular choice
among local residents. They flock here for the views, the ribs
and the friendly surroundings. Lines can be long on the weekend, so be prepared. Bring a Russian novel to pass the time.

Scott's Harbor Grill. 121719 South West Bayshore
Drive. (231) 922-2114. Just down the road from the
Apache Trout Grill, it is a popular place as well. You might
even see former Michigan Governor William Milliken, a
hometown boy, dining there.

Green House Café. 115 E. Front, downtown.
(231) 929-7687. An excellent choice for a light lunch right smack in the middle of the downtown shopping district. Salads, sandwiches, soups and such.

Horizon Bookstore. 243 E. Front, downtown.
(231) 946-7290. More than a bookstore, this is a café, a performance hall and an after dark hangout. The heart of the local literary scene.

Cousin Jennies Gourmet Cornish Pasties. 129 South Union. (231) 941-7821. Cousin Jenny is the name given to women from England's Cornwall region. (Cousin Jack is the male equivalent.) The Cornish gift to Michigan cuisine is the stuffed pie known as a pastie. Usually the filling is meat but there are variations. This is Traverse City's best example of the tasty treat.

Sleder's Family Tavern. 717 Randolph, just west of Division St. (U.S. 31), west of downtown Traverse City. (231) 947-9213. The oldest restaurant in town, and one of the oldest in Michigan. It dates from 1882, still has the original bar, and recent renovations have only enhanced the Victorian ambiance. The stuffed animal heads on the walls are a house tradition, but whether or not you want to join in and kiss the moose is entirely up to you.

Kiss the moose!

Moomer's. 7263 N. Long Lake Road, west of the city. You know Moomer's ice cream has the real deal because a herd of cows is grazing right in back of it. How authentic can you get? Open all year.

You can't beat homemade ice cream, right from the cows

Speaking of ice cream, another local favorite is **Bardon's.** Located at the corner of Garfield and U.S. 31, and one block from Bryant Park and the bay and immediately next to the Civic Center, it has been in business for over 50 years. From spring through fall, great ice cream at great prices and two hot dogs for a buck. Beat that!

Bardon's, a very popular place in summer

The House. 826 Front Street. (231) 929-4917. Specializing in innovative breakfasts and lunches, the House is popular with many doctors and nurses at Munson. You will get excellent food here in an atmosphere that is very unique, as you really are eating in a house. Opened in the summer of 2004, the owner was previously the executive chef at 310 and the Boathouse---very nice credentials.

Grand Traverse Pie Company. 525 W. Front, west of downtown. (231) 922-7437. With all that fruit hanging from the branches of the surrounding orchards, how can you resist a place with a name like this. A small menu of salads, quiches and chicken pot pie complements the main attraction, featuring thirty varieties of pies, including four kinds of cherry pies alone.

Burritt's Fresh Market. 509 West Front, in the same parking area as Grand Traverse Pie Company, and as locals will tell you, across from the fire station. (231) 946-3300. Looking for fish? Burritt's has one of the biggest selections north of Grand Rapids. Thirty five selections, daily, of fresh fish with scallops, clams, oysters, seven choices of shrimp, plus four varieties of smoked fish, including the local's favorite, smoked white fish.

Bay Bread Company. 601 Randolph Street, one block north of the intersection of Division and Munson. (231) 922-8022. You will have to look for their big red sign, but if you are looking to select from over 30 different varieties of bread with the oven is right next to the register, plus a nice selection of sandwiches, scones and cinnamon rolls, this is a great choice.

CITY WALKS

Traverse City: Sixth Street and Old Town

There are several pleasant residential thoroughfares in the neighborhoods off downtown Traverse City. But none are quite as evocative as Sixth Street.

Lined with homes that were built to be showplaces, and a park that runs down to the banks of the Boardman River, this is the perfect place for a walk into the past.

The stroll also will give you a close encounter with the

city's great visionary, Perry Hannah. Sixth Street was his baby. He intended it as a neighborhood for the business and political leaders of Traverse City, a suitable expression of the wealth and prestige flowing into the place in the 1890s.

Hannah did not altogether trust the aesthetic sensibility of these newly-made fortunes, though. So he set forth the rules for those who wished to build their homes on Sixth; right down to the depth of setbacks from the street, architectural design and the kinds of trees to be planted there.

Hannah saw his development more as a private association rather than a conventional city street. But the rigor with which he enforced these stipulations resulted in the harmonious setting that remains more than a century later. The entire neighborhood is on the National Historic Register, which protects it from the sort of change that Hannah would have deplored.

Leave the car at the **Grand Traverse Heritage Center,** at Sixth and Pine. This is the former Carnegie Library, built in 1904 on land donated by Hannah. Since the library closed in 1998 (a new facility has since opened on Woodmere Avenue), it has been converted into a resource center for organizations dedicated to preserving the city's history and a museum.

The Perry Hannah house, located on Sixth street

Perry Hannah's home is right across the street, at
305 Sixth. It is a mansion befitting the most powerful man
of his times in northern Michigan. He built it in 1893, a
14,000-square foot monument to his towering achievements.

It is now a funeral home, which some may find ironic
or even poetic. But the Jonkhoff family, the present owners,
have preserved it as an historic treasure, right down to the
paneling and chandeliers. They even offer tours of the
Queen Anne style house, with advance notice.
Call (231) 947-6347. It is the only home in this neighborhood open to the public.

When you leave the **Perry Hannah House,** turn left on
Sixth. You will immediately encounter one of the inter-
twined family relationships that are also a hallmark of this
neighborhood. The home at 319 Sixth was built by
Hannah's daughter-in-law, Elsie Raff, for her father in
1905. The senior Raff was already a resident of the neighborhood, being the town postmaster and a custom tailor.
But his daughter was now in the big chips and thought her
dad would appreciate the gesture.

Next door, at 325 Sixth, is the **"Vinegar John"** Morgan
house, built in 1893 by the owner of the first fruit canning
plant in town. The gardens here are magnificent and worth
a long, slow look. Morgan's son, nicknamed **"Wild Bill,"**
was a rather colorful individual who served as mayor, and
was a convicted bootlegger. He ended up in the Northern
Michigan Asylum.

At 333 Sixth is the home of **Cuyler Germaine,** one of
Hannah's most trusted executives. Germaine actually
moved in here 10 years before the boss and his choice may
very well have influenced Hannah when it came to pick his
model neighborhood.

The house at 502 Sixth, at the western limit of the
Historic District, was built by the superintendent of that
facility, Dr. James Munson. He never lived there, though,
preferring to reside at the Asylum and used this as an
investment property.

At 501 Sixth is the house **Elsie Raff** moved into when

she married Julius Hannah in 1896. The initials **ESBE** are carved above the front door, and probably have something to do with the original builders, the Smith-Barnes family.

As you retrace your route on the other side of the street, you will come to **Hannah Park,** the perfect place to stop for a rest. Looking down at the gently flowing Boardman River, it is, perhaps, unkind to recall that this was once the site of a rollway, where logging trains dumped their cargo for water transport. But that was an improvement over its original function as the town dump. That was all long gone when Hannah moved in, of course.

Detailed descriptions of all the homes in this neighbor-hood are available in a free brochure, **"Welcome to Central Neighborhood Historic District,"** at the **Heritage Center.**

You can finish up this walk by continuing to Union Street, where a right turn takes you into the middle of Old Town. There are several intriguing small shops in the vin-tage buildings along the 300 and 400 blocks of S. Union, most of them selling home and garden adornments.

The original Carnegie Library

Downtown and the Bayfront

Traverse City's business district is neatly tucked into the elbow of the Boardman River as it makes a sweeping curve before emptying into Grand Traverse Bay. There are about 150 shops and restaurants along a roughly five-block stretch of Front Street, between Wellington on the east and the river on the west.

The district's longtime anchor, Milliken's Department Store, an enterprise that gave the state one of its longest-serving governors, is gone. It closed in 2001, in its 128th year at the corner of Front and Cass. But two years later, the property was reopened as **Milliken Place,** and now houses a variety of small businesses. That is more in keeping with the present character of this downtown. It is a place of individualistic, mostly locally owned shops: Galleries, clothing stores, eating places. It's an eclectic mix and a great place for browsing, either aimless or directed.

Start at the corner of Front and Union. There are meters along Front Street but spaces may be in short supply. The better choice is to leave the car at a city lot, on the far side of one of the bridges (which, by the way, are great places to watch the fall salmon run) across the Boardman, between Front and U.S. 31.

As with so much of historic Traverse City, this corner bears the imprint of the Hannah-Lay partnership. The imposing red brick bank building with the circular clock tower on the northwest corner was originally their bank, the chief financial institution in town. After its founding in 1868, it financed much of Traverse City's growth. This structure, which replaced the original, was erected in 1902. The clock is one of the town's most enduring landmarks.

Directly across Union is the former **Hannah-Lay Mercantile.** After its opening in 1883 it was not only the biggest department store in the north but grandly claimed to have more goods in stock than Chicago's Marshall Field. As with its erstwhile rival, Milliken's, it now houses a variety of smaller stores.

As you walk along the south side of Front, you will pass the **City Opera House,** halfway down the block. Built in 1891 (another pet project of Hannah's), the ornate, three-story red brick theater building became the community gathering place. Not only plays and concerts, but town meetings and an occasional indoor sports events were held here. It was turned into a movie house in 1920, but shut down after World War II and stood vacant for several years.

The historic Opera House

When interest in the city's cultural heritage revived in the 1980s, it reopened on a limited basis. A non-profit organization was formed to raise funds for a full scale restoration and an $8 million program began in 1999. The first phase was completed in 2004, but the official grand opening is not scheduled until 2007. Meanwhile, the Opera House can be visited on an irregular basis. Call (231) 941-8082 to check on the status of access to the interior.

Across the street on the next block is the **State Theatre,** another of the projects that is transforming downtown into a cultural and performance center. This was once the premier movie house in town, as you can tell from the old marquee. But as with its senior partner, the Opera House, it is now a live performing arts venue, run by the **Interlochen Center for the Arts.** Its location next to **Horizon Books,** with its ongoing program of poetry readings and appearances by authors, makes this ground zero for the local literati.

There are still stores here that are intended to serve downtown office workers. But as with many places that have a buoyant tourist industry, Traverse City's central core is increasingly geared to the seasonal shopper; one who is looking for a knick-knack or serious piece of art that will allow them to carry away the texture of the place. There are dozens of places along the 100 and 200 blocks of East Front that fit that description.

Look in at the **Cherry Stop**, at 211 E. Front Street. It offers cherry gifts in every imaginable form, from candy to coffee and from juice to jams. It is, quite literally, a taste of Traverse City to take home.

Rather than walking back along this street, turn towards the bay on one of the cross streets, instead, and look for the stairs to the river walk. This **boardwalk along the Boardman River,** with boats tied up at the rear of Front Street's shops, is a pleasant alternative. It was slightly controversial when first proposed. Some environmentalists felt it would wipe out whatever remained of the river's natural setting in this area. Nonetheless, the walk went in and complaints diminished.

At Cass Street there is a pedestrian tunnel beneath busy Grandview Parkway to reach **Clinch Park**. This green space along the bay is a big part of what gives Traverse City its special appeal. In a matter of steps you can walk from the heart of downtown to beaches, a marina and a zoo.

The **zoo**, encircled by a miniature steam train, is one of the city's signature attractions. It was founded in 1932 as a place to exhibit animals native to northern Michigan. Kids are delighted by the otters and beavers, shiver at the bears and wolves and marvel at the winged raptors. While the little train and animal displays are aimed at a young audience, adults will be charmed by the place, too. It is a small facility and easily walkable.

Afterwards, you may want to stroll out to the recently refurbished marina for a look at the boats and wonderful views over the west arm of the bay to the hills of the Leelanau Peninsula.

As you continue west along the water, you will see a rather striking 19th Century industrial structure right ahead. This is the former Traverse City Gas Company. Its current function also involves illumination, but of a much more ancient variety. Since the 1970s it has been the home of the **Candle Factory.**

The shop inside offers a wide assortment of candles for sale and also gives visitors a chance to see them being made. More than that, it is a fascinating peek at the insides of a century-old industrial building, when they built for keeps.

With the aroma of scented candles in the air, this is a good place to end this walk.

Interlochen

The National Music Camp is not strictly a city. Well, let's be honest. It's not a city at all. But it is a fine place for a short walk. Especially if you like to stroll accompanied by the sound of music.

Pull into the main entrance off M-137 and try to leave your car in one of the first lots on the right. You will then walk across the road and into **Osterlin Mall.** This is the central assembly point for refreshment, information and buying souvenirs.

Ahead and to the left is the **Kresge Auditorium.** It's the hall with all the flags out in front. Each one represents the homeland of someone in the student body. It was dedicated in 1948 for the purpose of promoting **"world friendship through the Universal Language of the Arts."** That motto still appears at the back wall of the stage.

The covered outdoor arena seats 3,929 people and is the featured venue for the Symphony Orchestra and appearances by guest artists. It backs up to Green Lake, visible through the open rear of the stage.

Just to the right of Kresge is the **Bowl,** the oldest structure in the complex. It dates from the very first summer the camp

A performance at the Bowl, the oldest structure at Interlochen

was held, in 1928, and is still used for traditional gatherings and performances of student orchestras, choirs and jazz ensembles.

Past the Bowl and behind to the left is the **Lewis Dance Building.** Visitors may observe classes in ballet and modern dance.

Retrace your steps to Osterlin Mall and turn left along Percy Grainger Lane. The first structure on the right is the **Visual Arts Building.** Exhibits by students and faculty are mounted here and change on a weekly basis. You may also observe art classrooms from the doorways.

Percussion marks your steps to the next structure on the left. The **Frohlich Building** houses the piano and drum classrooms and you will hear it long before you see it.

Interlochen's two other performing halls are straight ahead on the right. **Corson Auditorium,** the larger of the two, seats 972 for dance and chamber music, while the **Harvey Theatre,** just beyond it, has a 174-seat studio theatre.

Turning back to the center of the camp you soon will pass **Dendrinos Chapel,** built in 1991. It is used for religious services and recitals on the magnificent 45-rank Aeolian Skinner pipe organ. Continuing the walk along the **Giddings Concourse** will then bring you back to the starting point of this excursion.

This would be an excellent time to walk into the Scholarshop to take away a memento of your visit, or better yet, buy tickets for an upcoming performance.

COUNTRY DRIVES

One of many views on Old Mission

Old Mission Peninsula, M-37 and Peninsula Drive

This is a classic northern day trip, from the middle of Traverse City to the very tip of the scenic, bountiful peninsula that rises from its core.

Watch for the M-37 turnoff from U.S. 31, about one mile east of downtown. This road heads right up the spine of Old Mission Peninsula as Center Highway. We'll come back that way, but on the journey up we'll stick to the water route. So bear left on Peninsula Drive at the first stoplight after leaving U.S. 31.

The drive opens out on splendid views across the bay's west arm to the Leelanau Peninsula. The people who live around here like that view, too, as you can tell by the fine homes they built on the far side of the road. The bay side remains largely unencumbered with nothing to interfere with the sight lines.

Soon the homes become more widely separated and the peninsula reverts to orchard and farmland. **Power Island,** once owned by Henry Ford, will soon come into view. It is now a county park, largely undeveloped, with lots of secluded beaches and hiking trails and accessible only by private boat.

About two-thirds of the way up you'll come to a deep inlet, known as **Bowers Harbor.** Two of the restaurants mentioned in the Eating Out section are located here, and there is also a small winery just off the highway on Bowers Harbor Road.

Peninsula Drive cuts away from the water here, but remain on this road to **Old Mission Road.** Turn right as it cuts across the peninsula to the town of Old Mission, site of the original settlement by Rev. Peter Dougherty. There is a replica of that log church and the **Old Mission General Store** to wander through. It has a soda fountain, bakery, deli, a ghost or two---just the sort of things one would expect in a 160-year old store.

Another great restaurant on Old Mission

Keep heading north out of town, take a left at Tompkins, and then right on M-37. The road leads to the end of the peninsula and the **Old Mission Lighthouse,** which sits right on the 45th parallel, midway between the Equator and North Pole.

The old light, which warned mariners for 63 years until it was decommissioned in 1933, is a favorite subject for artists and photographers. Sitting on a rocky bluff at land's end, it is surrounded by parkland. It is, in fact, used as a residence for employees of this township park and is not open to visitors. If you walk down to the water, however, the view back up to the light is a great photograph.

You are now about 22 miles north of Traverse City and the quickest way back is right along M-37 (Center Highway). You will pass a string of farm markets along Center Highway, offering the fruits of the season. There are also no fewer than three wineries; from north to south they are **Chateau Chantal, Chateau Grand Traverse** and **Peninsula Cellars.**

You can also stop at the **Mapleton Market,** the store that all the locals use throughout the year—with an incredible selection of items for life on the peninsula. You can also take a right on Nelson Road which will take you to visit **Walt's Antiques,** a fascinating place for browsing. There is also a scenic turnoff from Center Highway at Bluff Road. You can see for miles, so bring your camera.

So in other words, the drive back can be as tasty and slow as you care to make it.

U.S. 31, Traverse City to Antrim County

For most of its run through this area, highway 31 is in sight of the water. Development sometimes cuts off the view, but there are also several public parks along the route where you can stop off for a swim or a picnic. (See Beaches.)

The run up the eastern arm of Grand Traverse Bay is especially nice. Just past the Grand Traverse Resort watch for the picture book views across the fields to the big red barn that marks Amon Orchards, with the water just beyond M-37 and M-113.

M-113. This drive, especially in the fall, is one of the

A typical countryside scene found in the Grand Traverse area

most colorful around. No water, but just hill after hill of brilliant color. Take U.S. 31 south, past Chumm's Corner, take a left a few miles out and follow the highway markers.

SHOPPING

A walk through downtown Traverse City will lead you to the area's most concentrated assortment of shops. Many of them are the boutique variety, locally owned and, in many cases, locally crafted. The four blocks that make up East Front Street's shopping district are crammed with these places and it will take a good day's work to search them out.

A short list of places to poke into might include:

Belstone, at 321 E. Front (231-946-0610), which describes itself as a contemporary gallery in fine art, jewelry, glass, metal and wood.

Watermelon Sugar, at 153 E. Front (231-929-7426), showcasing area artists and crafters.

Wooden Gallery, at 116 E. Front (231-941-0823), which is heavy on the medium the name indicates.

DeYoung's, at 234 Front Street (231-946-8021), is a wonderful store to pick up your supplies for art projects for the occasional summer rainy day—an impressive selection to choose from.

Vintagey, at 141 E. Front (231-933-4207), for fans of retro high fashion.

Fetish, at 139 E. Front (231-941-0205), for women who go ga-ga over "Sex and the City" style shoes.

Federico's Design Jewelers, at 158 E. Front (231-946-4252), is the most innovative jewelry designer in the area. There is usually a goldsmith at work in the window and many of the pieces were crafted right on the premises.

Two other jewelers are close by:

Martinek's, 217 E. Front (231-946-4664), the oldest in the area, and **Miner's North Jewelers,** 222 E. Front (231-946-8528) with a a wider price range.

Wilson Antiques, around the corner at 123 S. Union (231-946-4177) has 50 dealers showing on four floors.

One of the finest art galleries in the area (mentioned in the Eating Out description of the Old Mission Tavern) is **Bella Galleria.** It adjoins the restaurant at 17015 Center Road, on the Old Mission Peninsula (231-223-4150). There is a sculpture garden here as well as galleries in glass, acrylic, bronze and paintings.

If you are a fan of jerky (and, honestly, who isn't?), a visit to **Deering's Meat Market** has to go on your list. The place has been in the business of preparing beef and turkey jerky, and sausages, for a century. Located at 827 S. Union Street, in the Old Town area (231) 947-6165.

Maxbauers, just down the street, at 407 S. Union (231-947-7698), is a favorite meat market and grocery store that locals go for their meat. You won't be disappointed. The selection is great, and in the summer, this place is crowded, the line can be out the door.

One of the great places for rockhounds in this area is **Korner Gem,** at 13031 South Fishman Cove located in Brewery Creek (take a left off of M-22 at the McDonalds, across from West Bay Marina). (231-929-9175). Owners Kevin and Chenina Gauthier have rare finds for sale, will polish the rocks you come in with and even give you some tips on where the best hunting sites may be. They also make beads with local stone for jewelry.

Another collection of shops is in the concourse of **Grand Traverse Resort** (231-938-2100). The emphasis is on sports wear and the prices, as you might expect in an upper-end resort, are not in the bargain range.

Grand Traverse Mall

Grand Traverse Mall (231-922-7722) is the largest enclosed shopping center in the North, with more than 70 retail outlets, predominantly national chains. It is anchored by Marshall Fields, JC Penney, Target and T.J. Maxx. The mall is on U.S. 31, south from downtown, at Airport Road.

Horizon Outlet Center (231-941-9211) features another grouping of 25 national stores, including Bass, Dansk, Van Heusen, Old Navy and the other usual suspects. It is also on U.S. 31, south of the city.

Grand Traverse Crossing specializes in big-box stores and there are about a dozen of these mammoth national retailers there. The mall has also won commendations from local land use groups for its attention to landscaping, architecture and minimally invasive environmental impact. It's on South Airport Road, just east of the Grand Traverse Mall.

Cherryland Center, another shopping area

Wineries

Wineries are popular on Old Mission

All four wineries on the Old Mission Peninsula have tasting rooms and gift shops to carry away some of the local vintages. You can't go wrong with the Rieslings, which have won medals at national competitions since 2001.

From south to north they are:

Peninsula Cellars

Peninsula Cellars, at 11480 Center Road (231-933-9787). This winery was started in 1994 by the Kroupa family on their 150-year old cherry farm. It is noted for its dry Gewurtztraminer and white cherry dessert wine. The tasting room is in a former schoolhouse.

Chateau Grand Traverse, at 12239 Center Road (231-223-7355). This was the pioneer winery on the peninsula and remains the largest, with 80 acres of vineyards. Recommended are the Johannisberg Reisling and Gamay Noir. There is a small inn here and the winery also offers tours of the operation.

Wineries and views on Old Mission

Bowers Harbor Vineyards, at 2896 Bowers Harbor Road (231-223-7615). The Stegenga family describes this as a boutique winery. Their site, overlooking a lovely inlet on the bay's western arm, promotes good conditions for growing Vinifera grapes, with Chardonnays and Rieslings the top choices.

Chateau Chantal, off Center Road, at Smokey Hollow and Boursaw Roads (231) 223-4110. The most elaborate of the area wineries, with a full-service B&B, a calendar of wine seminars and Jazz at Sunset concerts

in summer. It successfully emulates a European winery. It produces first-rate Chardonnays and Rieslings and even a sparkling wine blend with Pinot Meunier grapes.

Most of these wineries are open 11 a.m. to 5 p.m. daily and from noon on Sunday. In the winter months, Peninsula Cellars is only open Thursday through Sunday, noon to 5 p.m.

Spas

While **Grand Traverse Resort** is noted primarily for its golf and other recreational activities, its spa is one of the finest in the Midwest. There are 100,000 square feet of sybaritic indulgence here, with twenty-one treatment areas dispersed over fifteen separate rooms.

Saunas, aerobics area, yoga, two indoor pools, four whirlpools. It also claims to employ the healthful benefits of locally grown cherries. Room rates and reservations at (231) 938-2100.

When the men are out fishing, golfing, women have some great choices. There are three excellent choices for an impressive city day spa experience. In town is **Pavlova,**

The entrance to the Grand Travese Resort

which provides European-style treatments for hair, nails, skin and massage---everything from seaweed wraps to aromatherapy. It's right downtown, at 114 S. Union St. (231) 941-5707.

Just a few blocks from downtown, **Impres'** (231) 941-9094, 901 W. Front, is very elegant and classy from the moment you walk in; and **Epiphany** (231) 933-8010, 518 E. Front, a full innovation concept spa and salon, and **Salon West,** (231) 933-9378, 824 W. Front. You won't go wrong with any of these.

Farm Markets

If you don't come away with some of the locally grown food products, you really haven't done Traverse City. This is a city in an orchard and the farm stand is a ubiquitous feature of a ride down any nearby road.

The Michigan Land Use Institute publishes a booklet called "Select a Taste of Traverse Bay," a guide to local farm foods. Most of them offer pick your own during the season. A sampling would include:

Amon Orchards, Acme, at 8066 U.S. 31 (231) 938-9160. Cherries in all possible forms, pumpkins and baked goods. U-pick for tart and sweet cherries in July.

Buchan's Blueberry Hill, Old Mission, 1472 Nelson Road, off Peninsula Drive (231) 223-4846. U-pick berries from August to mid-October.

Edmondson Orchards, Old Mission, at 12414 Center Highway. Cherries, apricots, plums, apples, summer veggies, jellies and maple syrup. U-pick until 5 p.m., July to November.

Elzer Farms, Old Mission, 12654 Center Highway (231-223-9292). U-pick for strawberries, raspberries and cherries. Also asparagus, pies, jellies and other fruit for sale.

Mrs. Yankee's Peaches, Williamsburg, off M-72 north on Elk Lake Road, to 8844 Palaestrum Road. Succulent late summer peaches, near the shore of Elk Lake. U-pick from the third week of August through Labor Day.

Rennie Orchards, Williamsburg, east off U.S. 31 on Angell Road, then north, at 11221 Munro Road (231)264-8387. Cherries in July, third week of September through October for apples and pumpkins. Hayrides in the fall, too.

Hoxsie's Orchard Hills Farms, Acme, at 6578 M-72 (231) 267-9087. Weekend U-pick for cherries and apples, July through October.

Other interesting farm markets include:

Downtown Farmers Market is held every Wednesday and Saturday, from mid June through September. It sets up in the parking area on the south side of Grandview

Parkway, between Union and Cass streets. Look for the large awnings.

Olds Brothers Maple Syrup, Kingsley, Garfield Road, south from Traverse City. They also sell sweet corn in season.

Groleau's Farm Market, southeast of the city, at Four Mile Road and Hammond Road. A big operation, just outside of town, with all sorts of cherry products, maple syrup, tomatoes, cider and eggs.

Seventh Hill Farm, Old Peninsula, at 16975 Peninsula Drive. Specializing in leeks and several amazing varieties of garlic, starting in late August.

Youker Farm Market, Grawn, on M-37, south of the U.S. 31 intersection. A bit out of the way, but loaded with good stuff, from cherry products to asparagus to cabbage and winter squash. The stand is staffed daily, from May through October.

MUSEUMS AND SIGHTSEEING

Dennos Museum Center, 1701 E. Front Street. 10 a.m. to 5 p.m., Monday to Saturday; 1 p.m. to 5 p.m. Sunday. Admission $4 for adults, $2 for children. (231) 995-1055.

On the campus of **Northwestern Michigan College,** this museum has one of the finest collections of Inuit art in existence. There are more than 900 pieces of sculpture and prints, a vivid expression of the art of the Native people of the Canadian North.

There are changing exhibits in the galleries and a sculpture court with work by Michigan artists. The Center, which opened in 1991, also contains a science area with hands-on displays.

The Inuit collection was begun by Bernie Rink, an early

library director at Northwestern Michigan College. His widespread and rather eclectic choices in reading not only awakened a fascination for this kind of art, but also with wine-making. Rink became convinced that grapes could flourish in this climate. In the early 1980s, he established Boskydel, on the Leelanau Peninsula, a pioneering vineyard in this area.

Music House Museum, Acme, 7377 U.S. 31 North. Open May through October; Monday to Saturday, 10 a.m. to 4 p.m., Sunday, noon to 4 p.m. Admission $8. (231) 938-9300. Guided tours only.

The star of this collection of unusual antique musical instruments is a Mortier dance hall organ. It is a massive, magnificently carved music-making machine that once throbbed out its tunes for revelers in Ypres, Belgium in the 1920s. It was restored and can still be played.

Player pianos, music boxes, church organs and rare devices, such as a mechanical violin, are displayed. Opened in 1983 in a former dairy barn, the museum also features the organ from Detroit's defunct Cinderella Theatre. All the exhibits are shown in nostalgic settings of 19th Century stores, a saloon and a theater.

Grand Traverse Heritage Center, 322 Sixth Street. Open Monday to Saturday, 10 a.m. to 4 p.m. Donation. (231) 995-0313.

This is the city's history museum in the middle of its most historic street. The Sixth Street area is described in the City Walks section. The museum, in the former Carnegie Library, features exhibits on the lumbering era, railroads, Great Lakes shipping and the city's pioneers.

Grand Traverse Commons, Eleventh Street, west of U.S. 31 South.

On the grounds of the former Northern Michigan Asylum, a village within the city is taking shape. This is very much a work in progress, although you can already visit Building 50, the centerpiece of the restoration. As mentioned in the Dining Out section, an Italian restaurant, Trattoria Stella, has opened in the basement of what once was the main hospital building. Plans call for a mixed use development of residences, offices and a small commercial district. Much of it will remain as parkland, and it is already popular in that form with local hikers and bird watchers.

Joseph H. Rogers Observatory. Brimley Road, off Garfield, (231) 995-2300. Call for the public viewing schedule.

Built with private funds on a hillside south of the city, the observatory is operated by Northwest Michigan College. Its viewing schedule coincides with predictable heavenly phenomena and the experience is exceptional.

BEACHES

Beaches are a popular draw in Traverse City

They don't call this area Michigan's Riviera for nothing. The beaches on both arms of Grand Traverse Bay and a number of inland lakes are tops in the North. Private resorts have made a special effort to bring in sugar sand in recent years, but the public facilities also feature comfortable beach blanket areas.

On the Bay

Traverse City State Park. U.S. 31, on the east arm. Maybe the best in the area. A full 700 feet of sand with a bathhouse. Standard State Park entrance fees apply.

Clinch Park is just a short walk from downtown, beneath Grandview Parkway (U.S. 31) by pedestrian tunnel, at Cass Street. There is 1,500 feet of frontage along the west bay, with restrooms and life guards in summer. The park also contains a marina and zoo. Because of its location, it attracts crowds, but the convenience is hard to beat.

West End Beach is a little further along the west bayfront, at the foot of Division Street, where U.S. 31 makes its turn to the south. Hassle free parking, lots of space and restrooms.

Elmwood Township Park is a bit to the north, along M-22, just across the Leelanau County line. It adjoins a marina and has a playground and picnic area.

Bryant Park is a terrific place for kids. It has a good beach, a playground, picnic area, grills and lots of shade. On the west arm, right where M-37 turns north to enter Old Mission Peninsula.

East Bay Park is another excellent choice for families. It is a bit quieter, off the highway, on Front Street at East Bay Blvd. Follow Front east from U.S. 31, just past the entrance to Northwestern Michigan College. Lifeguards, playground, picnic area and a sandy, shallow bottom.

There are three beaches on **Old Mission Peninsula. Bowers Harbor Beach** is near the boat launch on Peninsula

Drive and offers swimming in the sheltered inlet of the west arm. Across the peninsula, on the east arm, is **Haserot Beach Park,** just past the town of Old Mission, on Forest Ave. This is the sandiest location on the Peninsula. There is also a small swimming area in the rather rocky northern tip of the peninsula at **Old Lighthouse Point Park.**

Old Mission Lighthouse is worth the drive

There are three beaches on the east arm in the Acme area. Closest to the city is **Tony Gilroy Township Park,** right off U.S. 31 North. There are picnic tables.

Bayside Park is bigger and better equipped, with 600 feet of frontage, a bathhouse, playground and extensive picnic area. This is the best spot on this part of the bay. It is just south and west of the intersection of U.S. 31 and M-72.

Acme Township Park is a bit more secluded, sitting off U.S. 31, just north of Yuba Road.

Inland Lakes

Arbutus Lake is southeast of the city and there is a public beach with a playground on its northern end. Take Garfield Road south, then east on Potter Road and North Arbutus Lake Road.

Elk Lake is one of the largest inland bodies of water in the area. Whitewater Township Park gives public access near its southern end. Take M-72 to Williamsburg, north on Elk Lake Road, then west on Park Road. Picnic facilities, playground, boat launch.

Long Lake is another convenient excursion for Traverse City residents. It is due west of town, out Front Street, which turns into North Long Lake Road. Gilbert Park has a good sand beach, with picnic area and restrooms.

COUNTRY WALKS

Traverse City's enthusiasm for the vigorous, four-season outdoor life is a big part of what draws people to this community. It's the sort of commitment to getting around without a car that usually is associated with states in the West--- where shorts and backpacks are a familiar uniform. The attitude is a bit harder to find in the Great Lakes area, but the on-the-trail mentality abounds here.

The most extensive is known as **TART,** which stands for Traverse Area Recreation Trail. It isn't actually a walk in the country, but an eight-mile route across the Traverse City area with minimal interference from motorized traffic.

It begins on Bunker Hill Road, just off U.S. 31, on the east bayfront. There is a parking area at the trailhead.

It then winds west all the way across the city; past Traverse City State Park, a nature preserve, the north side of the airport, around downtown and into the waterfront area along Clinch Park and West End Park.

Hikers, runners, in-line skaters and cyclists can pick it up at several points along the way. There are additional parking areas at Three Mile Road, just west of the state park; at Barlow Street, east of downtown; at Clinch Park, and at the western terminus, the intersection of M-22 and M-72, at the Leelanau County Line.

You are never far from food or restrooms on this walk, and it is a decidedly non-strenuous excursion.

A lot more challenging is the **Vasa Pathway.** (There are two Vasa trails, but one is intended for mountain bikers. This one accommodates walkers and cross-country skiers.)

The trailhead is just a bit beyond Tart's eastern terminus; off Bunker Hill Road, on Bartlett Road, in Acme. This is hilly terrain and three trails loop around the area, ranging from three to sixteen miles in length. The scenery is spectacular, but the way is hard. Hikers must ascend ridges on this trip and it is not recommended for leisurely walkers.

Just south of the city is the 470-acre **Grand Traverse Natural Education Reserve,** with seven miles of trails of leading to hills, a river with whitewater rapids, and swamps. This is an incredibly varied facility, owned jointly by the city and county and managed by the Grand Traverse Conservation Facility.

There are five trails, accessible either from Keystone Road or Cass Road. Nearest to the city is **Sabin Pond,** with branches that lead to a viewing platform over the water or to a boardwalk through the marsh. The most rewarding, arguably, is **Oleson Bridge,** with paths that run alongside one of the few whitewater rapids in the Lower Peninsula. Other trails lead to ponds and marshes within the reserve.

The plant and animal life in this area is highly diverse and it is, in fact, hard to believe that you are so close to a heavily populated area.

Other local trails fall between these extremes.

Lost Lake Pathway, near Interlochen, will take you to the shores of Lake Dubonnet in Pere Marquette State Forest. This is an artificial body of water, created by damming a nearby creek. The trail runs along an abandoned rail bed, past blueberry bogs and stands of red pine. The parking area is north from U.S. 31, just west of the Interlochen turnoff, on Gonder Road.

There are also walking trails at the park surrounding the Old Mission Lighthouse. Three miles of developed trails lead to highlands commanding a view of the tip of the peninsula.

There are excellent hiking trails at Old Mission Lighthouse

Muncie Lakes Pathway runs along the Boardman River in Pere Marquette State Forest. Much of it is hilly and quite scenic. Experienced hikers should have no problems with the trail, although it's just difficult enough to test the novice. Follow Garfield Road south from the city, then east on Hobbs and Ranch Rudolf Roads. The parking area is just west of Rennie Lake Road.

In another part of the forest is Sand Lakes Quiet Area, which is the state's way of saying, "No motorized vehicles." There are 3,500 acres here, with a seven and a half mile trail loop past tiny lakes and thick woods. The more ambitious can try the trails that lead to the hilly interior. Access is south from M-72, just east of Williamsburg, on Broomhead Road.

There are also some short trails in nature preserves in the Grand Traverse Area.

Right in town is the **Reffitt Preserve,** an 83-acre area that abuts the Tart Trail at Three Mile Road. A 1.7 mile loop leads to a boardwalk and nature observation point.

Brown Bridge Pond Natural Area encircles a small lake created by a dam on the Boardman. Trails follow the bluffs above the water and stairs lead down to the lake itself. There are also viewing platforms for observing the scenery and wildlife, which may include eagles. The parking lots are near Hobbs and Ranch Rudolf Roads, south from the city by way of Garfield Road.

Near Long Lake, southwest of the city, is **Bullhead Lake Natural Area.** It is just south of Gilbert Park (see Beaches section).

Pyatt Lake is a pleasant excursion in the Bowers Harbor area of the Old Mission Peninsula. This is a 140-acre preserve with loop trails leading to the inland lake and a marsh observation point. Take Peninsula Drive to Neahtawana Road, then right on Pyatt Road.

Deepwater Point Natural Area, near Acme, is a slice of Grand Traverse Bay shoreline just opposite the massive Grand Traverse Resort. Turn towards the water from U.S. 31 on Shore Drive. The entrance is across from the Vos Elementary School, and the trail from there runs down to the water.

BIKING

The **TART, Vasa, Lost Lake, Muncie Lakes and Sand Lakes** hiking trails and pathways are also excellent biking routes. Access information to these trails is in the previous section.

The **Vasa Single Track Loop** is, however, reserved exclusively for mountain bikes. It runs 13 miles through the Pere Marquette State Forest and is owned and maintained by the Michigan Department of Natural Resources and the Michigan Mountain Biking Assoication.

Cutoff loops can shorten the distance to as little as 3 miles.

Through most of the route this is a level, family-friendly course and on weekends you will meet many such groups. A more challenging route, however, goes into the hills. This alternative path is clearly marked at Checkpoint 10 of the trail and on Vasa maps, which can usually be picked up at the parking lot.

The **Vasa Single Track** can be reached from the city by taking Hammond Road east to High Lake Road, then south to Supply Road.

A good idea is to hook up with the **Cherry Capital Cycling Club,** which organizes road bike rides on the Old Mission Peninsula and mountain bike roads on the Vasa trail. Call (231) 941-2453.

There are now five primary outlets for bike rentals, repairs and information in the city.

1. **McLain Cycle and Fitness,** 2786 Garfield Road. (231) 941-8855 and 750 8th Street (231) 941-7161.

2. **GT Cycle,** 3007 Garfield Road. (231) 941-4868.

3. **Brick Wheels,** 736 E. 8th Street. (231) 947-4274.

4. **City Bike,** 322 S. Union Street. (231) 947-1312.

5. **Modern Extreme Sport,** 925 E. Front Street. (231) 933-7873.
   Located near the Muncie Lakes Trail is **Adventure Rentals,** at 4272 Scharmen Road, just off Brown Bridge Road. Its primary emphasis is on winter equipment but it added a bike rental service in 2004. (231) 263-3724.

BOATING

The river runs along downtown Traverse City

This is about as good as it gets for boaters. There are dozens of launch sites along the shoreline of Grand Traverse Bay and the inland lakes.

Every one of the state forest campgrounds listed in that section of the book has launches. They give access onto the **Boardman River, Arbutus Lake, Lake Dubonnet** and **Spring Lake.**

Interlochen State Park has launch ramps on both Green and Duck lakes.

Elk Lake, the largest inland body of water in this area, can be reached from Whitewater Township Park; north from M-72 at Williamsburg on Elk Lake Road, then right on Park Road.

You can also access **Lake Skegemog,** which adjoins Elk Lake, by following Baggs Road north from M-72, just west of the Kalkaska County line.

The trip to **Power Island** provides one of the top boating adventures in the area. In the west arm of Grand Traverse Bay, the island was owned by the Ford family until 1944. It was then purchased by Ann Arbor philanthropist Eugene Power, who donated it later to the county. It is now a 200-acre wilderness reserve, with excellent beaches and some interior hiking trails. Just off its northern tip, there is the even-tinier Bassett Island, also accessible only by private boat. You can still discern the foundations of an old dance hall there. To camp on Power Island, call the County Parks and Recreation Department. (231) 922-4818.

Rentals

Sunset Watersports is the primary rental agency in the area, with a full line of ski boats, jet boats, jet skis and pontoon boats. Free delivery within 25 miles. (231) 932-1800.

Adventure Rentals is located in the inland lakes area of southeastern Grand Traverse County. It will deliver to "the lake of your choice" in the area for free. Three-person wave runners are the craft of choice. (231) 263-3724.

Blue Sky Rentals features jet skis, wave runners and free delivery within 15 miles. It is located in Traverse City, at 422 Rose Street. (231) 633-2584.

Moose Lake Rentals, at 3871 Altaire Drive, will bring its Sea Doo personal watercraft to your drop-off site. (231) 649-4518.

Canoes and Kayaks

Ranch Rudolf is a unique operation. It is a taste of the simpler life, the way northern Michigan used to be a generation or two ago. A small camping- and-motel resort on 195 acres, in the midst of the Pere Marquette State Forest, it caters to families more interested in outdoor activities than gourmet dining and cable TV.

It offers horseback riding, hayrides and a long assortment of sports options, including cross country skiing and snowmobiling in winter. Warm weather picks are the rental canoe and tube trips along the adjacent Boardman River. Trip lengths range from 90 minutes to 3 and a half hours and you don't have to be a guest to participate.

Ranch Rudolf is located at 6841 Brown Bridge Road, east from Michigan 611 (Garfield Road), south of the city. (231) 947-9529.

A similar, and even tinier, operation is the **Ellis Lake Resort.** It consists of 10 log cabins and a three-bedroom chalet on the shores of a quiet inland lake. The entrance is off U.S. 31, just east of Interlochen. It has rental canoes and rowboats. (231) 276-9502.

McLain Cycle (see Biking section) has kayaks and kayak carriers.

Modern Skate and Surf, at 925 E. Front Street, rents kayaks and wakeboards. (231) 933-7873.

FISHING

A top fly-fishing stream

Chinook. Lake trout. Brown trout. Steelhead. Muskie. Coho.

If it's swimming in the northern Great Lakes area, chances are excellent that you can land it here.

Dozens of guided charters are available for trips around Grand Traverse Bay, the Boardman River and Elk Lake regarded by some experts as one of the top five inland fishing lakes in the state.

To sum up, fishing is a big deal in these parts.

The **Boardman** is an outstanding trout stream, and during the spring runs of steelhead and salmon fishermen flock to downtown Traverse City to pull them right out of the water as it reaches the bay.

Brown trout is the prize at the river's upper stretch,

near the two campgrounds in Pere Marquette State Forest, Forks and Scheck's Place. It is also where the renowned Adams fly was invented, and some portions of the river can only be fished with flies.

Several fly-fishing outfitters run full and half day trips to the Boardman from Traverse City. The national company, **Orvis Streamside,** has an outlet in Grand Traverse Resort and it makes sure that you are also fashionably attired when you encounter the trout. (231) 938-5337.

Among the local services are **Hawkins Outfitters,** which makes a point of catering to kids, beginners and group outings. (231) 228-7135.

Northern Angler is actually situated along the Boardman, at 312 S. Union Street, in the Old Town district. It holds casting classes for novices right outside its doors and offers full and half day trips for trout and carp.

There are several high-tech charter operations working the bay. Biggest of them is **Pisces,** with four boats of between 30 and 35 feet in length and five electric downriggers. The crew also cleans, filets and packages the day's catch. In charge of the operation is Capt. Tiny Ray, with 25 years of experience on the bay. It sails out of Acme, off U.S. 31 (behind the Mountain Jack's restaurant on the east bayfront). (231) 938-1562.

A good choice on the west arm of the bay is **Showtime Charters.** The enticement here is that the **Apache Grill,** one of the area's most popular restaurants, will prepare a lunch from the morning's catch. Captain Sam Worden runs a 26-foot Triton for these trips. Its berth is located on M-22, near Grand View Road, just over the Leelanau County line. (231) 218-1494.

Another West Bay possibility is the **Big Kahuna,** which runs out of the Elmwood Township Marina, on M-22. It is a 33-foot Carver with an experienced Captain who proudly shows off the Coho trophies he has accumulated since 1996.

Elk and Skegemog Lakes are connected and it is near their junction that the lakes give up their muskies. The legendary game fish can run up to 40 pounds, but they are not easy to find. Off Skegemog Point is the favored fishing ground for the locals.

Elk is also noted for its lake trout, and the best place to try for them is off the western shoreline in the deeper water.

Public access to these lakes is very close to both recommended fishing areas. From M-72 at Williamsburg, head north on Elk Lake Road, and then east on Park Road to reach Whitewater Township Park; or head a bit further east on M-72 and turn north on Baggs Road to reach Lake Skegemog access.

GOLF

The natural features of the **Grand Traverse** terrain, the hills and gently rolling dales, make it ideal for more than growing cherries. Golf has taken powerful root here, too.

The range of opportunities run from a course that many experts regards as the most challenging in the state to pleasant, duffer-forgiving, nine-hole layouts.

Grand Traverse Resort. Acme. The Bear. The Wolverine. Spruce Run. (231) 938-1620.

The Bear is every bit as grouchy and dangerous as the name implies. Named for its designer, Jack Nicklaus, this is a tough proposition for even the most experienced. Terraced fairways, tiered greens, deep roughs and a web of traps and water guarding each approach, this is a course where no two holes play the same. That is precisely what Nicklaus wanted, using the natural features to constantly change the skills called into play. Signature hole of this destination course is the 13th, a 167-yard par three over water.

The Wolverine is also named for an ill tempered animal. But it is a far more forgiving course than its neighbor at the resort. Designed by Gary Player, its extra wide fairways accommodate a good deal of novice mistakes. The approach shots, however, bring ponds and traps into continual play and make the course an adventure for scratch golfers.

Spruce Run is the third course on the property and this is a more amiable course, about 700 yards shorter and much flatter. It is a fair test, though, and was the site of the Michigan Open Tournament before completion of the Bear. The course was designed by former University of Michigan golf coach, William Newcomb.

Expect to pay $140 for a peak season round, mid-June to mid-August, on the Bear and the Wolverine; $90 on Spruce Run. Resort guests pay slightly lower fees.

High Pointe Golf Club. 5555 Arnold Road, Williamsburg. (800) 753-7888. Across M-72 from Turtle Creek Casino.

High Pointe has consistently been ranked among the top 100 public courses in the country since 1993 and *Links* magazine rated it one of the top 10 courses built in America in the 90s. Its diversity is part of the charm. The front nine is a Scottish-style links, with heather and bunkers that seem to draw in the wind. The back nine becomes a thickly-wooded hillside course with views over the bay. The architect, Tom Doak, is regarded as a bit eccentric, but with the mitigating factor of genius, leads to great design. He is now considered one of the world's best, and High Pointe was his first creation. A lot of his creativity is showcased here.

With a course rating of 73.3, High Point trails only the top two Grand Traverse Resort courses in this area. Weekend peak season fees are $69; twilight rates after 3 p.m.

Elmbrook Golf Course. 1759 Townline Road, Traverse City. (231) 946-9180. South on Garfield Road, then east on Hammond Road.

This is one of the older public courses in the area and also one of the most convenient, just a few minutes' drive from downtown. Elmbrook opened in 1964 and it plays along the hills on the southern edge of town, with views of the bay in the distance. Its nifty features are sand traps shaped like the Great Lakes guarding the 3rd green and majestic stands of mature hardwoods along the fairways. Rates during peak season are $49.

The Crown. 2430 West Crown Drive, Traverse City. (888) 921-2975. From U.S. 31 South, head left on Silver Lake Road.

This is a new course built across gently rolling terrain, the focus of a planned residential community, southwest of the city. It's a favorite with local residents who regard it as a fair test at a reasonable price. Peak season weekend fees are $55.

Interlochen Golf Club. 10586 U.S. 31 South, Interlochen. (231) 275-7311.

A mature course with beautiful North Country scenery and also a great value. The 12th hole, in particular, is a dandy. It's a 530-yard par 5 with water on the right of the fairway and guarding the green, and a marsh behind the green. Players must choose their clubs carefully on this course. Peak season weekends are priced at $37.

Cedar Hills Golf Course. 7525 Cedar Run Road, Traverse City. (231) 947-8237. West on Front Street to Cedar Run Road, to just past Strait Road.

A good course for families; at least, on the front nine, which is all par 3s. The back nine gets into the hills and is somewhat more challenging. The entire course is a par 58. Fees are $15.

Bay Meadows Golf Course. 5220 Barney Road, Traverse City. (231) 946-7927. West from downtown on Front Street, then continue on Barney Road.

Another course set up for families, with excellent practice and teaching facilities. There is a par-3 nine-hole course and another par-32 family course. Rates run from $15 on

weekends for the family course to $32 for the entire 18 holes.
Mitchell Creek Golf Club. 2846 Three Mile Road,
Traverse City. (231) 941-5200.
Nine holes over flat terrain, just south of the city. It
plays at over 3,000 yards and is a par 36. Rates are $18.

If you have connections to private clubs, there are three in
the area. The oldest, **Traverse City Golf and Country Club,**
opened in 1915, and is the most convenient, right in the center
of town on S. Union Street. The toughest, **Lochenheath** (is just
north of Traverse City), off U.S. 31, in a private development.
The highest rated is the **Kingley Golf Club,** just south of town.

WINTER SPORTS

There are some terrific downhill ski resorts in neighboring counties, but the big deal in the Grand Traverse area is
cross country. The system of trails in **Pere Marquette State
Forest** and along the **Vasa Pathway** are unsurpassed.

The **Vasa Trail** is east of the city, near Acme, with parking on Bunker Hill Road, off U.S. 31. Three loops of 3, 10
and 25 kilometers over a groomed course.

Lost Lake Trail is in the Lake Dubonnet area, just north
of Interlochen, with parking on Gonder Road, north of U.S.
31. There are 6.5 miles of trails through the natural area.

Muncie Lakes Pathway is reached from Scheck's Place
Campground or Ranch Rudolf, southeast of Traverse City
and east of Garfield Road by way of Brown Bridge Road.
There are 10 miles of trail with degrees of difficulty ranging
from beginner to advanced.

Sand Lakes Quiet Area is south from M-72 in
Williamsburg, by way of Broomhead Road. Just under 10
miles in trails, with a variety of loops. This is a non-motor-

ized area and the trails pass several small lakes--magical scenes in the middle of winter.

There are also trails at **Old Mission Lighthouse Park,** at the end of M-37 on the Old Mission Peninsula.

Grand Traverse Resort opens 2 kilometers of groomed trails across its property for a $5 fee.

Timber Ridge Campground and Nordic Center has 3 kilometers of trails that are also usable for night skiing. The rate is $5. It is south of the city at 4050 Hammond Road.

Hickory Hills has both downhill and cross country facilities. There are six lighted downhill runs, rated mostly as intermediate, with a vertical drop of 240 feet. The city-owned operation is due west of downtown, out Randolph Street.

Mt. Holiday reopened in 2003 after a two-year shutdown after being taken over by a non-profit community group. One of the first downhill runs in this area, opening in 1949, it now has 12 slopes for skiing and snowboarding. This is, above all, a friendly gathering place that is proud of the fact that 20,000 local youth learned to ski here. It is just east of the city, out Holiday Road from U.S. 31, past Five Mile Road.

Snowmobiles

The trails in this area are among the most extensive and best marked in the north of Michigan. The **Boardman Valley Trail System** runs for 81 miles through Pere Marquette State Forest and offer links to neighboring trails in Kalkaska and Wexford counties.

Best place to start is at **Peegeo's Restaurant.** It's at 525 High Lake Road, southeast of the city from Hammond Road. This is the starting point for much of the eastern section of the trail system, designated as Route 5, and the official headquarters for the area snowmobiler association, the

Snow Spiders. You can pick up some maps and some tips on routes, along with some hot food and a place to park.

Other options for picking up the eastern spur are **Dollar Lake and Fife Lake** staging areas. Dollar Lake is at Supply Road and Williamsburg Road and Fife Lake is further south, at the intersection of M-186 and Pierce Road, just off U.S. 131.

Ranch Rudolf (see description in the Boating section) lies right on this route and is an excellent place to stop for relief and refreshment.

Main staging area for the western loop, which is designated as Route 510, is **Hoosier Valley,** located just south of the M-37 intersection with U.S. 31 at Chums Corner. This is a less-traveled route than Route 5 and that makes for a more solitary experience and a faster ride. It hooks up with the eastern section just east of the town of **Mayfield.**

There are snowmobile rental facilities at **Peegeo's Restaurant. Blizzard Rentals** can be reached at (231) 929-1777. Another possibility is **Snowblitz Rentals** at (231) 932-1800. It is located on M-72, near the Turtle Lake Casino, at High Pointe Golf Club.

OFFBEAT SIDE TRIPS

Tall Ship *Manitou* is a replica of the sailing vessels that once carried cargo through these waters. Built in New England in 1983, it was constructed as a passenger ship and at 114 feet in length it can comfortably hold 62 of them on its daily sailings.

With its 3,000 square feet of sail unfurled, the *Manitou* is a magnificent sight, and even better to feel beneath your feet. During the summer months it sails three times a day---noon, 3 p.m. and 6:30 p.m.---for two-hour trips around Grand Traverse Bay.

Wine tasting cruises are held on Tuesday evenings and

live music is featured on Wednesday evenings.

Best of all, the *Manitou* also has 12 cabins that can hold 24 overnight guests, with breakfast thrown in as part of the deal.

The *Manitou* sails from the west arm, off M-22, one-half mile north of the M-72 intersection. Reservations can be made at (800) 678-0383.

Nauti Cat. This giant catamaran is docked at the Holiday Inn, and is perfect for trips to Power Island. (231) 947-1730.

Grand Traverse Balloons offers a whole different outlook on the area. Its seven-story high hot air balloons go soaring above the bay and hills, depending on how the wind happens to be blowing that day. The route cannot be guaranteed.

There are sunrise and sunset flights and an experienced pilot is at the controls. Flights must be reserved in advance at (231) 947-7433. The assembly point is at the company offices, at 225 Cross Country Trail. Leave Traverse City on Three Mile Road south, then east on Potter Road to Cross Country. Passengers are then transported to the take-off point for the day.

The Grand Traverse Dinner Train runs fine-dining excursions through the Pere Marquette State Forest and Boardman River Valley. Since the tracks are owned by the State, route and time can vary, but they usually come in at about three hours and cover about 60 miles.

The meals are high quality and prepared during the course of the trip in the galley cars; no warmed-over airline food here. There is usually a beef, chicken or fish dish for the entrée and special dietary needs can be accommodated. Seating is at traditional four-person tables in the dining cars.

The train runs on Saturdays all year at noon and 6 p.m. When darkness comes early---in late fall, winter and early spring---halogen lights attached to the cars illuminate the passing scenery. In June, the train also operates on Tuesday, Thursday and Friday; in July and August, on Tuesday through Saturday; and during color season, mid-September through October, there is a daily schedule. Advance reservations are required. Call (231) 933-3768. The 2004 prices ranged from $68 for off-season runs to $79.95 during color season. Trains leave from the Traverse City depot at 642 Railroad Place, south of Eighth Street and east of Franklin Street, just south and east of downtown.

AFTER DARK

There is a surprisingly active music scene here. Well, maybe not too surprising when you calculate the number of young people moving into the area and the readiness with which many Detroit bands welcome a gig up north.

Union Street Station is the liveliest of the rock clubs in town, just south of Front Street, at 117 S. Union. It's become known as the place where visiting celebrities are most likely to turn up. Kid Rock has made it a few times, and in years when there is a hockey season members of the Detroit Red Wings appear here, too, during training camp. The athletes also like Dillinger's, right down the block. Call (231) 941-1930 for scheduled events.

The Loading Dock is a top venue for local rock bands, with the occasional guest from Motown. Sometimes the place goes Irish, with musicians on traditional Celtic instruments. An interesting mix. It's located at 205 Lake Avenue, just across the Cass Street bridge, at the southern edge of downtown. (231) 941-4422.

Li'l Bo's, the former hangout of Hall of Fame golfer Walter Hagen, also shakes the routine up a little with jazz on Monday nights to augment a rotating cast of weekend rock bands. It's at 540 West Front, near Division Street. The odd name is short for Little Bohemia, since the neighborhood once was populated largely by Czech laborers.

Away from downtown is **Streeter's** which features four different clubs under one roof. Ground Zero does hip-hop. Liquid Lounge is techno. There is also a billiards hall and, for the tradition-minded, a dueling pianos saloon. It's located at 1669 S. Garfield. (231) 932-1300.

For those who prefer cooler sounds, the top choice is **Poppycock's.** It's a restaurant that reaches out to the artsy bunch with lots of vegetarian dishes and pasta, and features jazz and blues after 9 p.m. In the heart of downtown, at 128 E. Front.

Just across the way is the **Shine Café** in Horizon Books, which features folk and alternative jazz artists on weekends. It's music that is generally unavailable elsewhere which makes it fun for those who enjoy going out of the mainstream. (231) 946-7290.

The major hotels, Grand Traverse Resort and Park Place, both feature live entertainment at night in quite scenic rooftop rooms. At Grand Traverse, it's the **Trillium Lounge** and at Park Place, the **Beacon Lounge.** Good choices for soft jazz and a late romantic interlude.

During the summer months, the patio at **Holiday Inn West,** where U.S. 31 widens into the Grandview Parkway, is a gathering place for music under the stars. The hotel also has live performers indoors in **Shimmers nightclub.** (231) 947-3700.

Old Town Playhouse is the long-established local theater group. Formed in 1960, the group moved into the former First Christian Church, at the corner of Cass and Eighth Streets, in Old Town, 12 years later. It puts on a full schedule of musical and dramatic performances on its main stage, studio and youth theaters. The subscription season runs from early September to early June. (231) 947-2210.

The State Theatre, in a converted movie house downtown, presents a schedule of shows by a resident theater group, Michigan Ensemble, and a number of visiting groups and artists. Interlochen has taken over some of the scheduling and plans an expanded season of events here. For the schedule call (231) 929-1424.

Casino

The Turtle Creek Casino, owned by the same Native American band that operates Grand Traverse Resort, is four miles east of the hotel, on M-72, near Williamsburg. This is a 39,000 square foot facility with more than 1,200 slots and 25 table games, including several varieties of poker. There is a slots tournament on Tuesday nights and live entertainment in the Sands Showroom on weekends. Two restaurants. (888) 777-8946.

RAINY DAYS AND KIDS

Traverse Area District Library is a fine new facility with a great schedule of summer programs aimed at children. There is a Wigglers Fun session on Wednesday and Thursday mornings, and ongoing musical and photographic programs. It is located at 610 Woodmere Avenue, south from Eighth Street, east of downtown. The library is next to Hull Park on the shores of Boardman Lake. (231) 932-8500.

The mainstay downtown movie house, the State, is now a cultural center. But there are 19 screens at two shopping mall multiplexes. Ten are at Grand Traverse Mall, at U.S. 31 and Airport Road. (231) 941-0820. The others are at

the **Horizon Cinema,** at the Horizon Outlet Center, just a
bit to the north on U.S. 31. (231) 933-6394.

Great Lakes Children's Museum contains exhibits on
the ecology and history of the Lakes, geared to the level of
youngsters. There are displays on waves, shipwrecks as well
as interactive exhibits and art shows. It is on the western
edge of downtown, at 336 W. Front Street, along the River
Walk and the Boardman River. Admission $5. Open 10
a.m. to 5 p.m., Tuesday through Saturday; Sunday, 1 p.m.
to 5 p.m. Also open Mondays during the summer months.
(231) 932-4526.

For rainy days, check out the indoor soccer complex,
Just for Kicks, which has the largest climbing wall in the
North. It is located at 160 Hughes Drive, south of the city
by way of Garfield Road, then east of Hammond Road.
Call (231) 933-7022 for open climbing times.

There is also open skating at **Centre Ice,** located southeast of the city, off Hammond Road between Three and Four
Mile roads. Call (231) 933-7465 for schedules and rates.

A better than average amusement complex for a drizzly
day is **Pirate's Cove Adventureland,** on U.S. 31, east of
downtown. There are two miniature golf courses, go-carts,
bumper boats and hoop shoots.

Kid's Kove is an exceptional recreational facility, part of
the Grand Traverse County Civic Center, on Kid's Kove, W.
Civic Center Drive, adjacent to U.S. 31, with entrances off
Eighth St. and Garfield, 231-922-4818. There are eight
baseball fields, two full basketball courts and two half
courts, and an incredible skate park that cost a $1,000,000
to build all surrounded by a nice encircling one-mile walk-
ing/running track. There are also a six-lane indoor pool, a
picnic shelter and an ice skating rink that is open September
to March. (231) 922-4818.

Near the end of summer, when the National Hockey League is operating, the Detroit Red Wings hold their training camp in Traverse City at **Centre Ice**. If you are a hockey fan, this is a great way to see your favorite players in a relaxed atmosphere.

In the summer there is a lot of volleyball activity right on the bay at **West End Beach**. There are numerous sand courts with games going on all day long. You can also count on an ultimate Frisbee game around 5-6pm on a small field right next to the tennis courts, where U.S. 31 runs to the bay. If there isn't a game that day, bring your racquet. A nice plus is that the courts are illuminated for night play.

Speaking of sports, **Minor league baseball** also is coming to TC, the Traverse City Beach Bums. The stadium for the Traverse City Beach Bums is being built out by Chum's Corner, south of town on U.S. 31. It is entirely financed by private funds, the Wuerful family, who must be baseball crazy. Opening Day is scheduled for 2006.

If you are visiting during fall colors season, you may want to head for the Friday night lights. High school football is a huge community event (with tv trucks at every game). All three local teams---Traverse City Central, Traverse City West and Traverse City St. Francis---play their home games at **Thirlby Field**. It's between on 13th Street and 14th Street at Wadsworth, south of downtown. Watch the newspapers for schedules.

ANNUAL EVENTS

February:

North American Vasa Ski Race. The Vasa Trail, one of Traverse City's great recreational assets, was named for a 16th Century Swedish king. Gustav Eriksson Vasa skied across the country to warn of an invasion by the Danes and to rally resistance. It was sort of a marathon on snow and his actions earned him the royal crown.

The commemoration of Vasa's heroism began in Sweden in 1922 with a race between two towns. The North American version dates from 1976 and is now a major event on the Nordic racing calendar, drawing many former Olympic participants. There are 10, 27 and 48 kilometer competitions over the Vasa course, which begins near Acme. Call (231) 883-8278 for exact dates and more information.

April:

Traverse Area Antiques Club Show. This area is an almost bottomless trove of late 19th Century items, many of them taken from lumber era mansions as they come down or are modernized. More than 60 dealers attend the annual spring show in the Howe Arena on the first weekend of the month. The Arena is in Civic Center Park, on U.S. 31 just east of Garfield Street. (231) 943-6459.

May:

Downtown Farmers Market. Off Grandview Parkway, between Union and Cass Streets. Better than a supermarket and twice as fresh. Every Saturday from May through October; Wednesdays, too, July through September. Opens at 8 a.m. to noon.

Blessing of the Blossoms. This was the modest origin of the cherry festival extravaganza of today and it is retained as a tradition on the Old Mission Peninsula. Just as the orchards are at their peak of pink, the fun begins. The actual clerical blessing takes place at the Chateau Chantal winery, but there are also special tastings of both wines and juices, and seasonal restaurant menus served up and down the peninsula. The third weekend of the month. (231) 223-4110.

June:

Bay Day Watershed Festival. A celebration of the Grand Traverse Bay area, its physical features and its nautical lore. Outdoor activities are centered around the ecology of the bay. The festival began in Clinch Park but has moved to the Great Lakes Maritime Academy, on the campus of Northwestern Michigan College. The date varies, but is usually early in the month. Call (231) 935-1514.

Old Town Crafts Bazaar. This is when Traverse City's most historic, and somewhat funky, neighborhood comes out to strut. Booths are set up along Union Street, between 5th and 8th. Last Saturday of the month. (231) 922-2050.

July:

National Cherry Festival. One of the top destination events in the country. Parades and band competitions; street entertainers and fireworks; cherries served in every conceivable form; air shows, Native American dances, the coronation of the Cherry Queen and, to top it all off, the cherry pit spitting contest. It runs for the first full week of July. Reserve a room well in advance if you plan to attend. Center of the action is Grandview Parkway and Union Street but there are events all over town. (231) 947-4230.

Friday Night Live. Every weekend starts with a street party in summer. Front Street is closed to traffic downtown and becomes a pedestrian mall for entertainers, vendors, games and dancing. Outdoor dining and lots of music. From late July through August.

Traverse Bay Outdoor Art Fair. A summer institution since 1961. The juried show is held on the Northwestern Michigan campus on the last Saturday of the month. (231) 941-9488.

August:

Antique and Classic Boat Show. The wooden boats begin tying up in the morning along River Walk, behind Front Street. There are usually around 50 of the classic craft on display. First Saturday of the month, 10 a.m. to 3 p.m. (231) 922-2050.

Northwestern Michigan Fair. A traditional harvest festival with a midway, carnival rides, harness racing, food and animal exhibits. All that good stuff that reflects an earlier way of life tied to the passing of the seasons. The fairgrounds are on M-37, south of Chums Corner, and the fair goes on during the second full week of the month. (231) 943-4150.

November:

The Iceman Cometh. Certainly the most evocatively named mountain bike race anywhere and easily the sloppiest. By the time it is held, on the first Saturday of the month, the iceman usually has already arrived and left a fine mess of slush and mud behind on this 27-mile course. The race begins in Kalkaska and ends at the Timber Ridge Campground and Nordic Center, south of Traverse City. Great fun for all but the bikers. (248) 922-5926.

December:

Festival of Trains. Among the top model railroad events in the Midwest. More than 50 different modules are set up at the Grand Traverse Heritage Center, on 6th Street, and the little trains run thither and yon in the imaginary landscape. An annual part of the mid-December holiday season. Call (248) 995-0313 for exact dates. There is a $4 admission for adults.

HOSPITALS AND URGENT CARES

Munson Medical Center (231-935-5000), whose cardiac doctors originally came from the University of Michigan, located off 6th Street. Munson also purchased the osteopathic hospital (231-935-8686), now called Munson Urgent Care, located immediately off of U.S. 31, just a few miles north of Garfield. Both have urgent care units.

There are two privately owned urgent care facilities. They are **Bayside Docs** (231-933-9150), open six days a week.

Also off U.S. 31, closer to town, the **Walk-in Clinic,** across from the Horizon Mall. (231 929-1234).